SAXOPHONE WORKOUT

EXERCISES TO BUILD TECHNIQUE & CONTROL

BY ERIC J. MORONES

Front cover illustration by Elwood H. Smith.

ISBN: 978-1-4803-5257-5

HAL•LEONARD®
CORPORATION

7777 W. BLUEMOUND RD. P.O. BOX 13819 MILWAUKEE, WI 53213

In Australia Contact:
Hal Leonard Australia Pty. Ltd.
4 Lentara Court
Cheltenham, Victoria, 3192 Australia
Email: ausadmin@halleonard.com.au

Visit Hal Leonard Online at
www.halleonard.com

CONTENTS

PREFACE

Saxophone Workout comes out of 25 years' personal experience with the saxophone. Here you'll find etudes that cover a wide spectrum of techniques, from the basics to intermediate level to advanced. With daily practice that includes use of a metronome and tuner, this book will provide noticeable improvement in the mastery of your horn. The exercises are designed for the trouble spots of all the instruments of the saxophone family – soprano, alto, tenor, baritone.

NOTES FOR USING THIS BOOK

All the scales and exercises use the full range of the instrument. Most modern saxophones, and some older, have an added high F♯ key. Most of these exercises are written up to F♯. You can decide how high you want to practice – either to high F or high F♯. Please change any exercises accordingly. If your instrument doesn't have a high F♯ key, I have listed one fingering example. Practice or research other fingerings that work and feel most comfortable to you. Enharmonics have been used intermittently to help you learn and identify both note names: G♯/A♭, A♯/B♭, C♯/D♭, F♯/G♭, etc.

Always use a metronome at a comfortable tempo. I suggest starting all exercises slowly. Of course, you may start at whatever tempo is comfortable, but speed up only when you can play the exercise cleanly and flawlessly and with good tone.

Try to memorize these patterns/exercises, learning them away from the book. Using mental practice versus reading helps you learn the etudes better for mental and fingering practice. Eventually, you can use the book as a reference on an "as needed" basis.

Alternate high E and high F front fingerings (non-palm-key fingerings) are variously referred to as alternate, forked, or plateau fingering. The term "forked" is used in this book.

Practice all exercises using the various articulations shown below:

CHAPTER 1
RHYTHMS

Rhythm is what sets the pulse of music, determining the placement of sound in time. The basic rhythmic units are the whole note, half note, quarter note, eighth note, and 16th note – and their corresponding rests. Along with these, the rhythms given below are generally the ones you will see in music of all genres and style periods. Master the ones below – how they are played, sound, and counted – and you will be able to sight read anything and play quite efficiently.

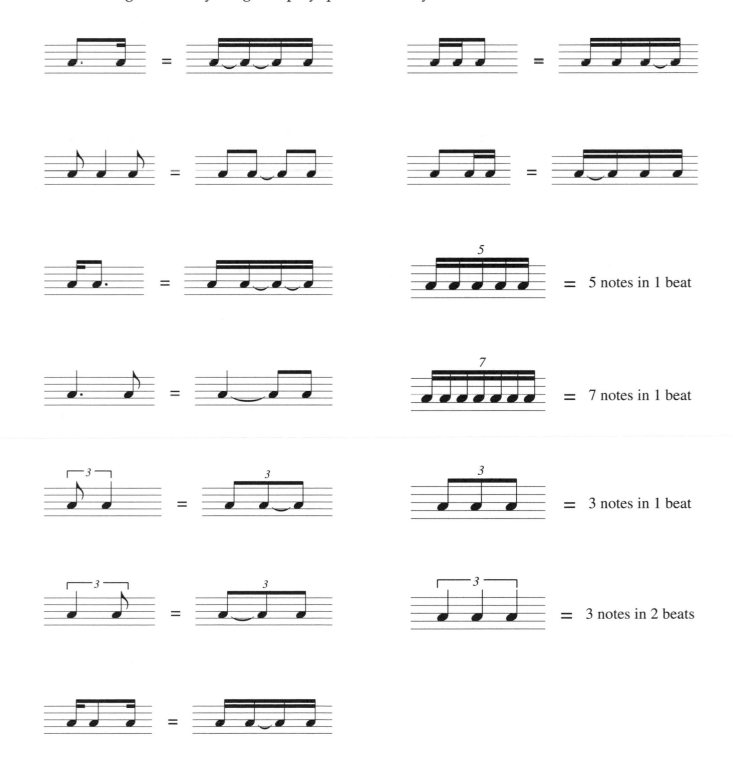

This exercise utilizes a variety of rhythms. Practice with a metronome, making sure each rhythm is played correctly and in time.

CHAPTER 2
TIME SIGNATURES

Various time signatures are used throughout music, with 4/4 (common time) the most used and comfortable to play. Practice each exercise below, fully understanding how each individual rhythm is played and counted. If you are confident of all these rhythms in their respective time signatures, you will greatly improve your music reading skills.

CHAPTER 3
ARTICULATIONS

Articulations tell us how individual notes are to be played within a phrase or musical passage. In the Preface (page v), you were given various ways of slurring notes together or separating them with a staccato articulation. Along with staccato, we have other means of articulation: tenuto, accent, and marcato. These are shown below.

Staccato: The note is to be played shorter than notated. Staccato marks may appear on notes of any value, shortening their performed duration without speeding the music itself.

Tenuto: A note should be played for its full value, or slightly longer; it may also indicate a slight dynamic emphasis.

Accent: The note is played louder or with a harder attack than surrounding unaccented notes. Accents can appear on notes of any duration.

Marcato: The note is played somewhat louder or more forcefully than a note with a regular accent mark.

The following melody incorporates all four of these articulations, as well as a set of slurred 16th notes. Practice with a metronome to ensure a steady beat.

This A major tune adds triplets to the rhythmic mix. Practice slowly at first, and gradually increase the tempo over the course of several days.

CHAPTER 4
LOW NOTES (Pinky Workout)

Practice all low-note exercises slowly. Use a metronome to ensure a steady beat and a tuner to make sure each note is clean and clear. Always leave your pinky on the keys, using the black-key rollers to move between notes. You can also experiment with shifting your left wrist downward. Use tonguing and slurring.

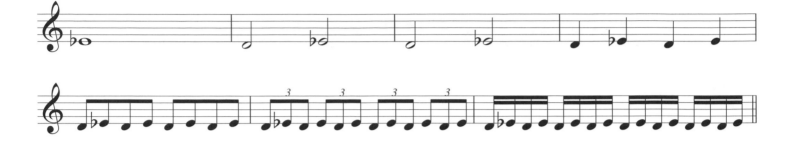

Practice this fingering also by leaving your right-hand ring finger D down.

Play each measure cleanly four times. Start slowly and increase the metronome setting over time. Use the various articulations shown in the Preface (page v).

CHAPTER 5
PALM KEY (High-Note Workout)

Practice with different articulations, as well as slurring.

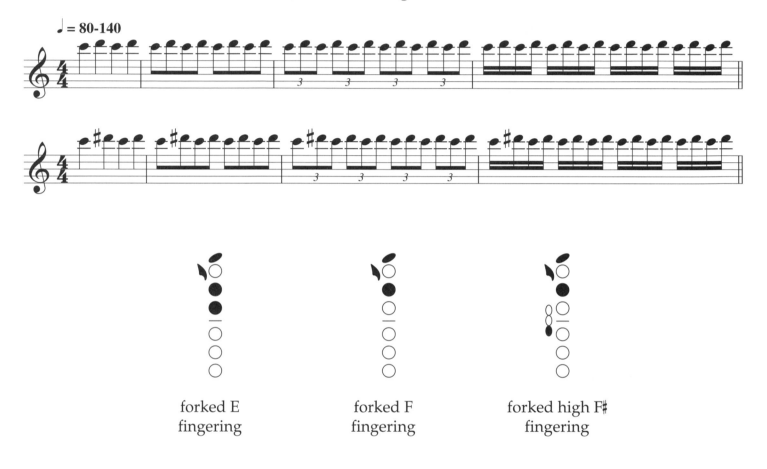

forked E
fingering

forked F
fingering

forked high F♯
fingering

Use forked and palm key fingering.

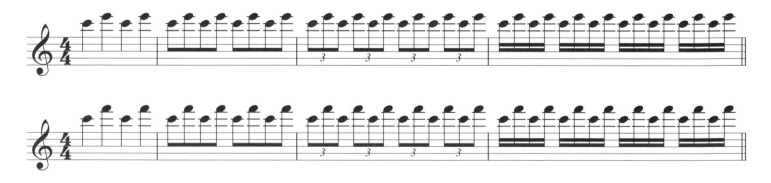

Practice all high F# exercises if your horn has a high F# key, or with suggested F# fingering.

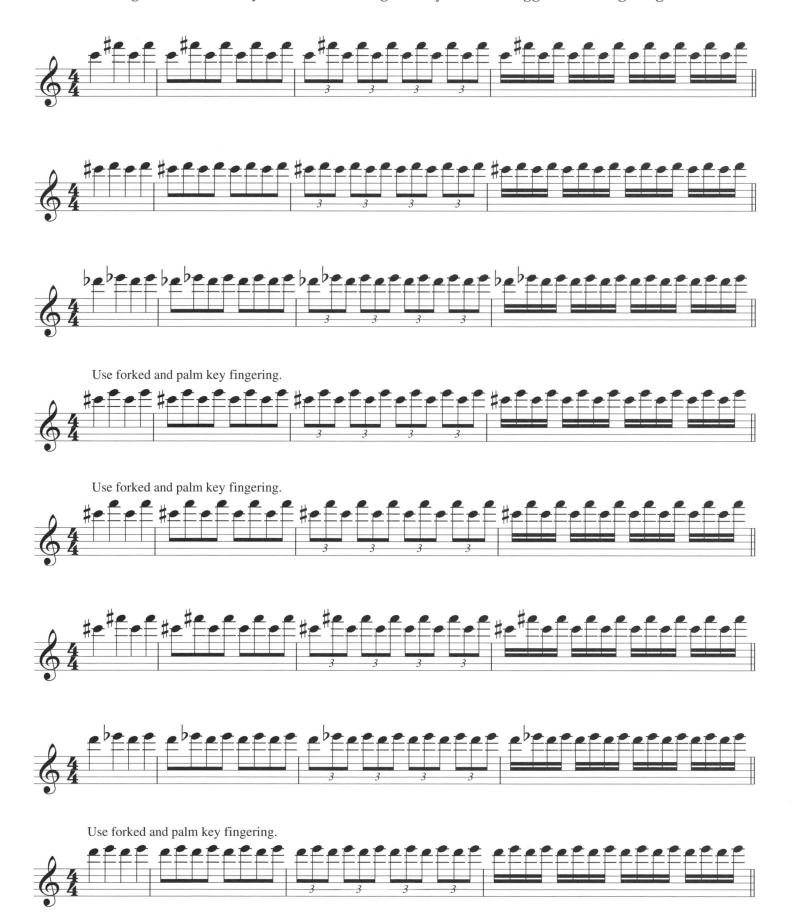

Use forked and palm key fingering.

Use forked and palm key fingering.

Use forked and palm key fingering.

Use forked and palm key fingering.

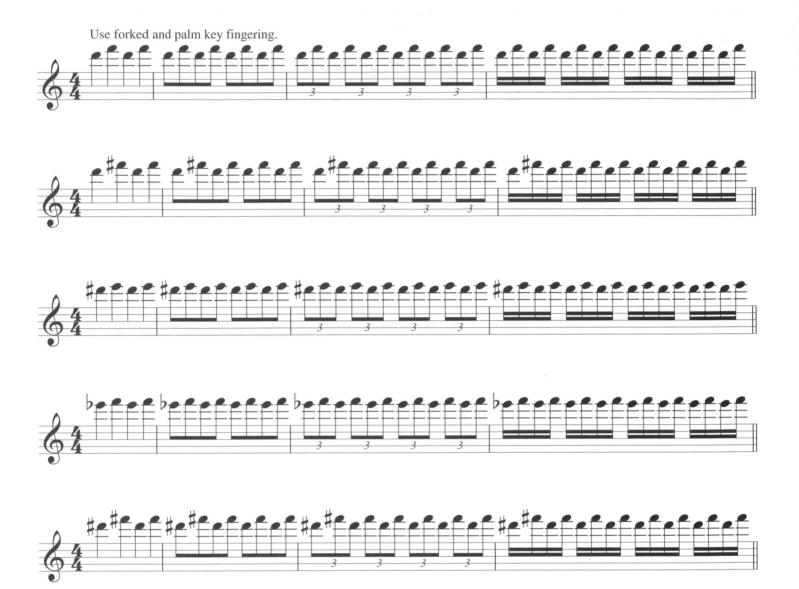

Use forked fingering also.

Play each measure cleanly four times. Start slowly and increase the metronome setting over time. Use the various articulations shown in the Preface (page v).

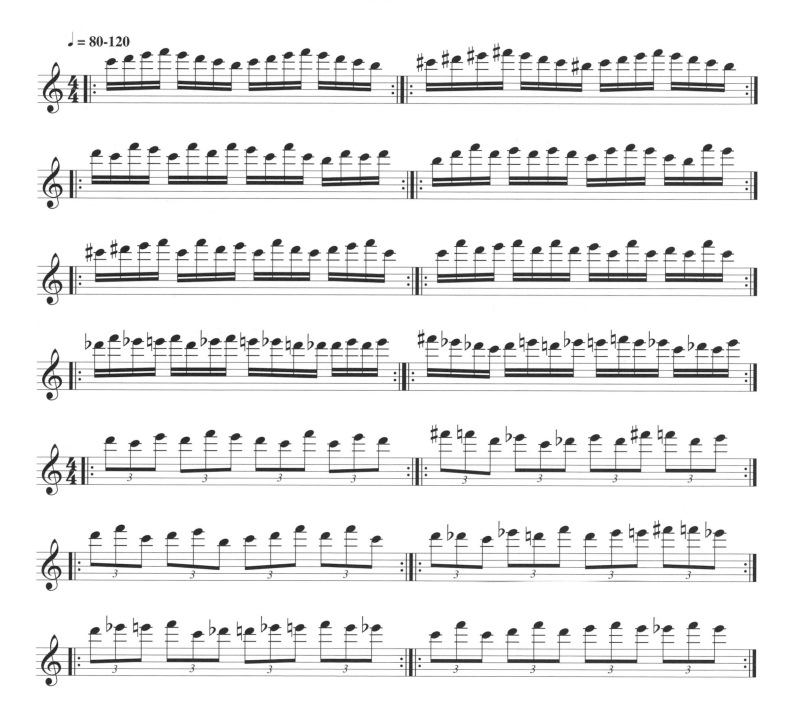

Use forked E and F throughout this exercise, practicing with various articulations.

CHAPTER 6
ALTERNATE FINGERINGS

The saxophone has several alternate fingerings for certain notes, making musical passages with those notes easier to play. Learning and applying these alternate fingerings will help you master the instrument.

Practice 1 and 1 B♭ (A♯) fingering throughout this exercise.

Practice 1 and 2 B♭ (A♯) fingering throughout this exercise.

Use low B fingering for A♭ (G♯).

C.

Use low B♭ for A♭ (G♯).

D.

Use low D♭ (C♯ fingering for A♭ (G♯).

E.

Practice with both 1 and 1 and side key B♭ (A♯).

F.

Use side C -

- ⌐   Use chromatic F♯ (G♭) fingering - - - -

CHAPTER 7
MAJOR SCALES

Start slowly and increase the metronome setting over time. Use the various articulations shown in the Preface.

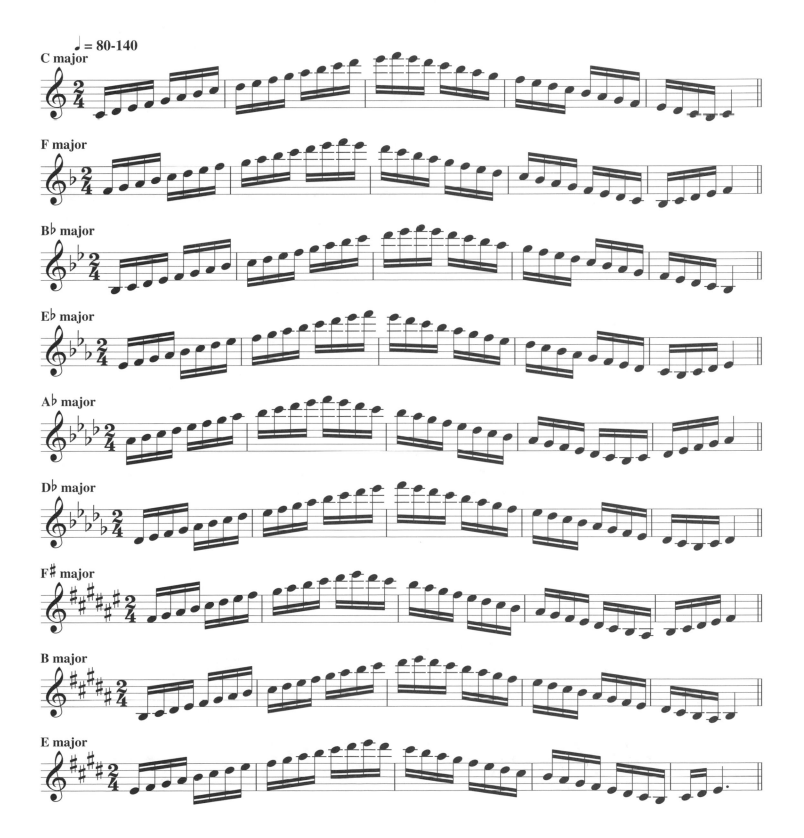

A major

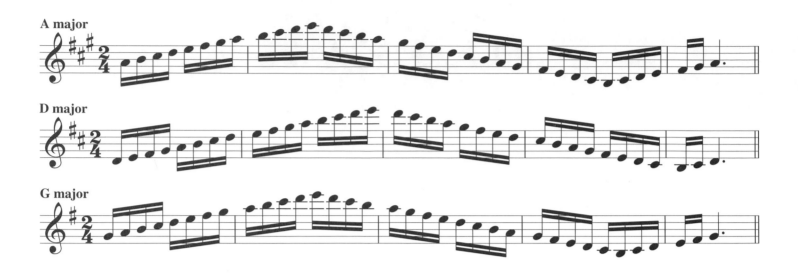

D major

G major

As you begin to work on these quintuplet scales, you may wish to start with a slower metronome setting. Remember to practice with differing articulations and phrasings.

C major

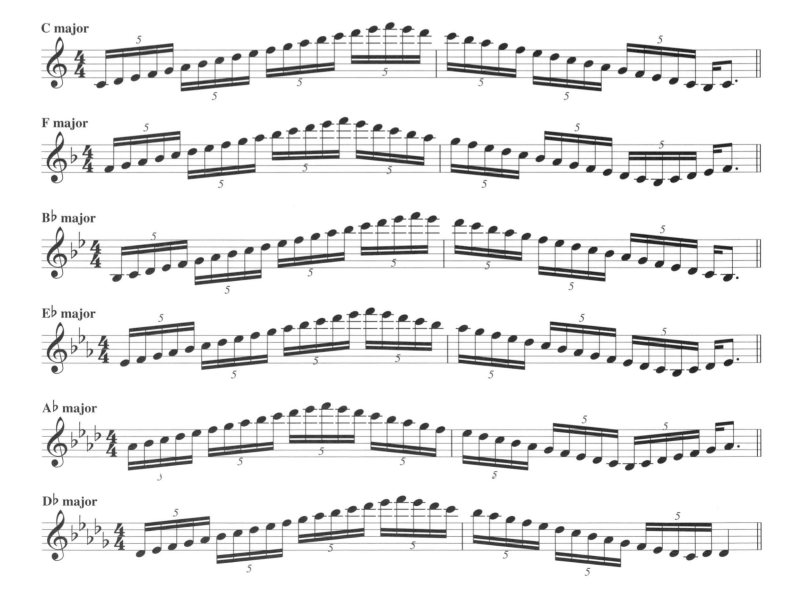

F major

B♭ major

E♭ major

A♭ major

D♭ major

F# major

B major

E major

A major

D major

G major

CHAPTER 8
MINOR SCALES

In Western classical music, there are three forms of the minor scale: natural, harmonic, and melodic. The natural minor scale is the sixth mode of the major scale. Harmonic minor and melodic minor scales are formed by altering certain notes of the natural minor scale.

Here's the familiar C Major scale:

The A Natural Minor scale starts on the sixth note of the C Major scale. It is known then as the sixth mode or the Aeolian scale.

Harmonic Minor has the seventh note raised.

Melodic Minor has the sixth and seventh notes raised ascending, but lowered back down descending.

Start slowly and increase the metronome setting over time. Use the various articulations shown in the Preface.

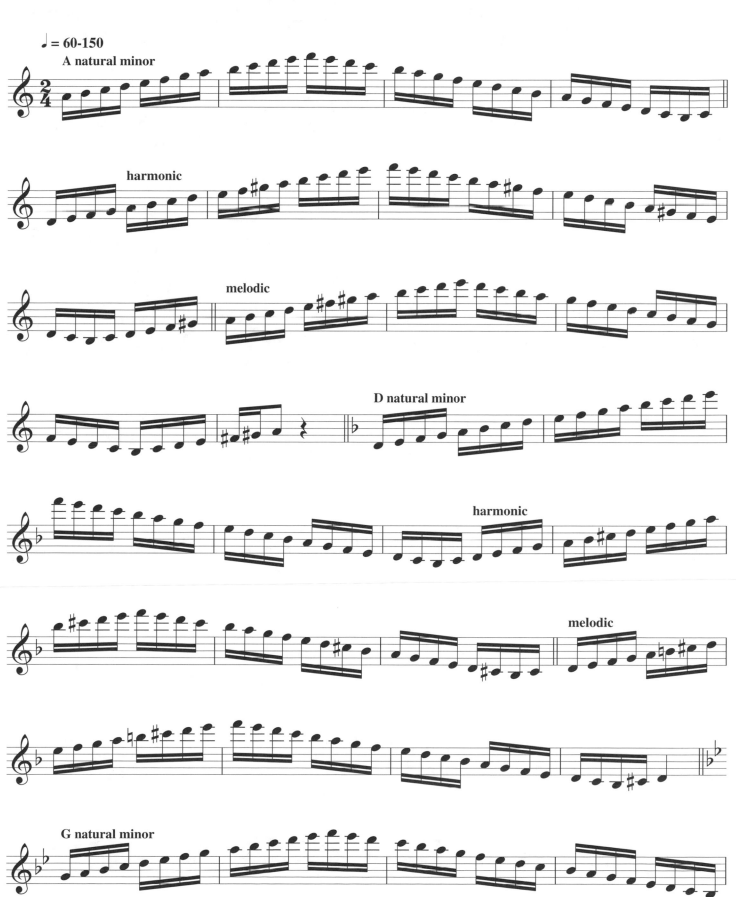

harmonic

melodic

C natural minor

harmonic

melodic

F natural minor

harmonic

melodic

B♭ natural minor

harmonic

melodic

E♭ natural minor

harmonic

melodic

G♯ natural minor

harmonic

melodic

C# natural minor

harmonic

melodic

F# natural minor

harmonic

melodic

B natural minor

harmonic

melodic

E natural minor

harmonic

melodic

CHAPTER 9
CHROMATIC SCALE & PASSAGES

Start these etudes slowly and increase the metronome setting over time. Use various articulations.

D.

E.

CHAPTER 10
BLUES SCALES & PENTATONIC SCALES

Blues scales and pentatonic scales are two types of scales based on the major scale.

A blues scale is based on the 1 (tonic), ♭3, 4, ♯4 (♭5), 5, ♭7, 1 (tonic) of any major scale, for a total of 12 possible blues scales.

A pentatonic scale (five notes) is based on the 1 (tonic), 2, 3, 5, 6, 1 of any major scale, for a total of 12 possible pentatonic scales.

The following etude presents the blues scales in the Circle of Fourths. As always, use the metronome, starting slowly at first and increasing the tempo over several weeks. Use various articulations.

This exercise presents the pentatonic scales in the Circle of Fourths. As always, use the metronome, starting slowly at first and increasing the tempo.

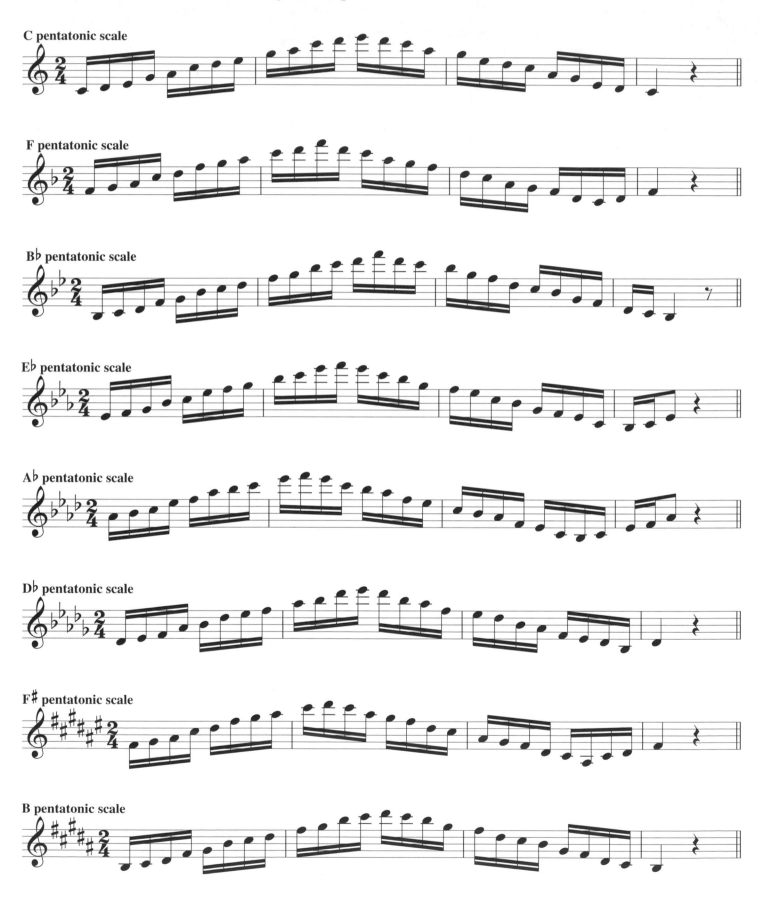

E pentatonic scale

A pentatonic scale

D pentatonic scale

G pentatonic scale

CHAPTER 11
CHORD ARPEGGIOS

This chapter presents five basic chords – major, major 7th, dominant 7th, minor 7th, and diminished 7th – in arpeggiated form. Begin in C major and follow the Circle of Fourths through all 12 keys. Use the metronome, employing differing articulations.

♩ = 70-120

C major — major 7th

dominant 7th — minor 7th

dim. 7th

F major — major 7th

dominant 7th — minor 7th

dim. 7th

B♭ major — major 7th

dominant 7th — minor 7th

dim. 7th

E♭ major

major 7th

dominant 7th

minor 7th

dim. 7th

A♭ major

major 7th

dominant 7th

minor 7th

dim. 7th

D♭ major

major 7th

dominant 7th

minor 7th

dim. 7th

A major major 7th

dominant 7th minor 7th

dim. 7th

D major major 7th

dominant 7th minor 7th

dim. 7th

G major major 7th

dominant 7th minor 7th

dim. 7th

CHAPTER 12
OCTAVE EXERCISES

Practice with a metronome, making sure to keep your jaw and embouchure still between the octaves. Keep your fingers relaxed at all times. Use a tuner to make sure each note is in tune and clear. Experiment with various articulations.

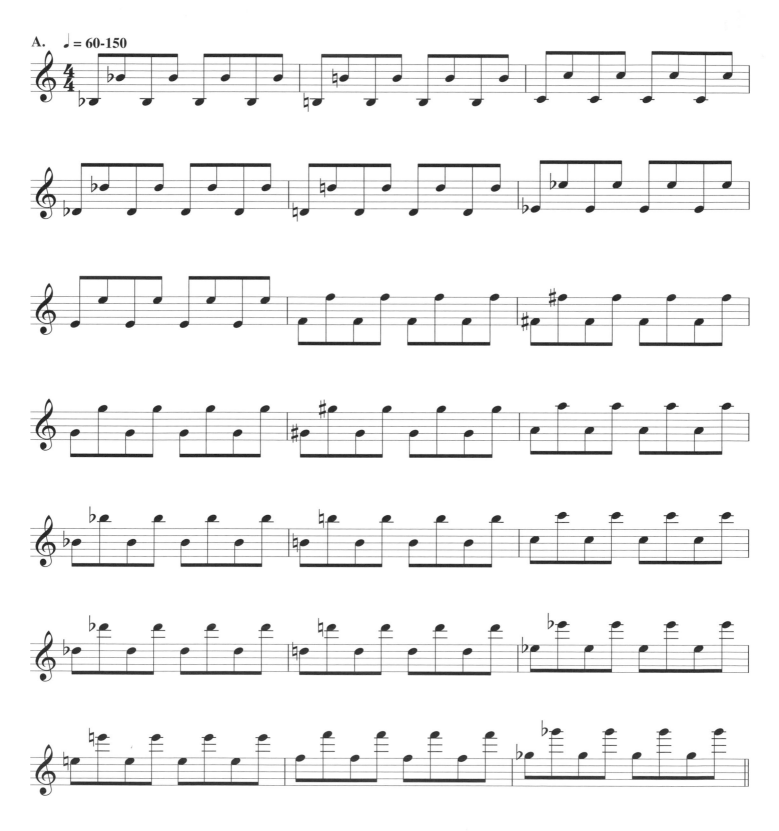

CHAPTER 13
HUGE INTERVAL LEAPS

Make sure that you do not move your jaw or embouchure between notes, and keep your fingers relaxed at all times.

C. 10ths

D. 10ths

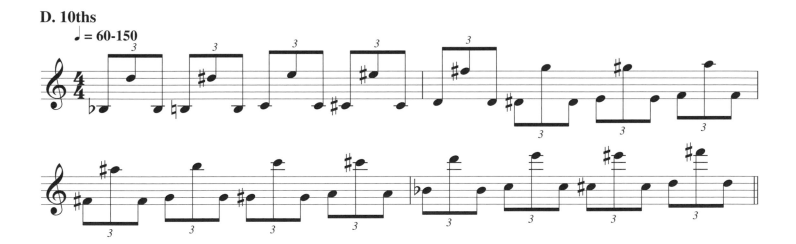

E. 11ths

F. 11ths

G. 12ths

H. 12ths

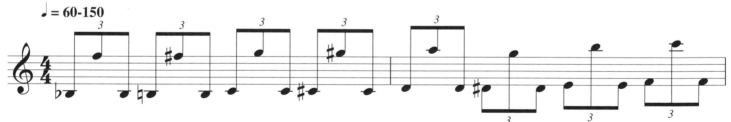

I. 13ths

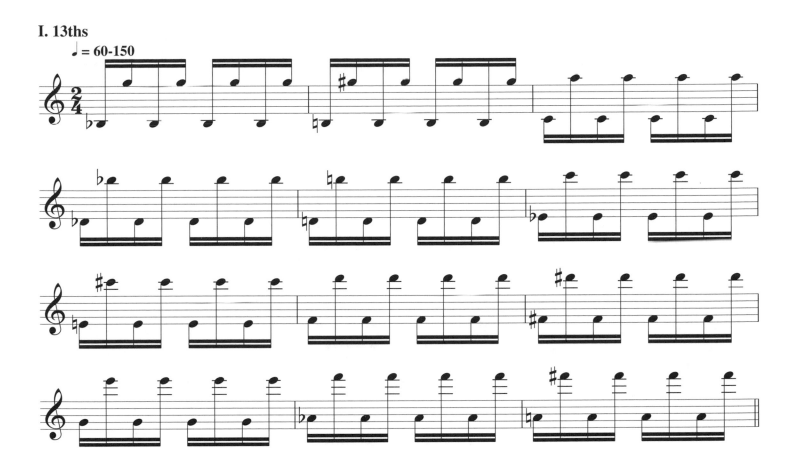

J. 13ths

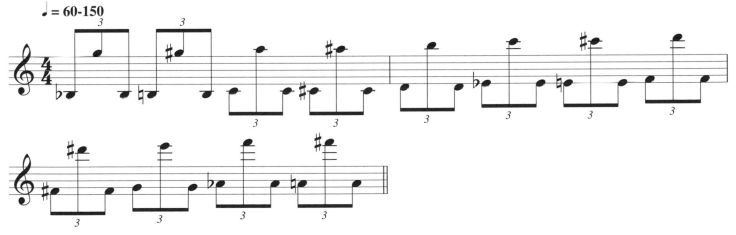

K. 14ths

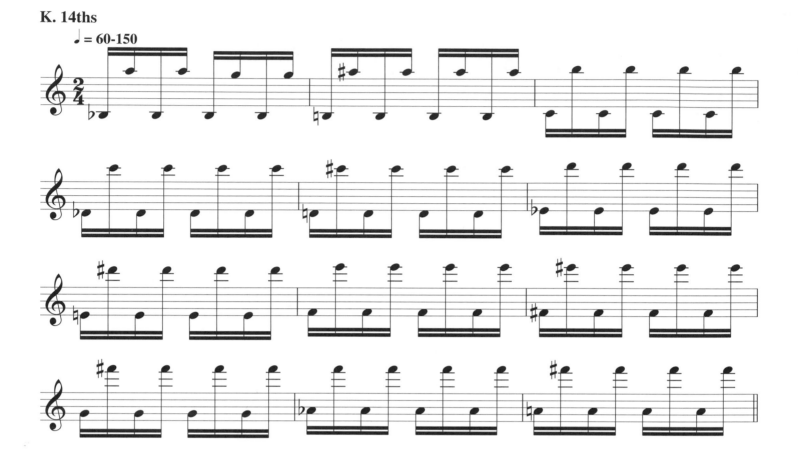

L. 14ths

CHAPTER 14
EMBELLISHMENTS

Embellishments (or ornaments) are notes or phrases that decorate a musical line. These are most often encountered when playing classical music. Below are some of the most common types of embellishments.

Trill: A rapid movement between a note and the note a whole-step or half-step above it. The trill (or "shake") may begin on the upper note or the main note, partly depending on whether its function is more melodic or harmonic.

Mordent: In its normal form, a mordent consists of the rapid alternation of the main note with the note a step below. This is also known as a lower mordent. The inverted (or upper) mordent is a variation in which the main note alternates with the note above.

Turn: An ornament consisting of the note above the main note, the main note, the note below, and the main note again. The Italian term for turn is *gruppetto*; the German term is *Doppelschlag*.

Grace notes: Ornamental notes printed smaller than the main text. These are notated several different ways, and may be played before the beat or on the beat, depending upon the musical context. Be sure to tongue grace notes, or the first note of several grace notes.

The following melody, in C major, incorporates the ornaments described above. Practice it slowly and expressively.

CHAPTER 15
OVERTONES

Overtones or harmonics are notes or frequencies higher than a fundamental (main) note. Not only are overtones excellent for making your overall embouchure and tone stronger, but they are vital for playing notes in the altissimo register (those above high F or F♯). To produce overtones on the saxophone, we finger a certain note (in these exercises, the low-note fingering) and aim to get a note (tone/partial) higher than the original note, without the octave key pressed.

Practice with strong air and a good reed. Experiment with tightening your throat and embouchure. Do not use the octave key on any of the low overtones. At first, the overtones may seem hard to produce, but with proper practice they will become easier. For more in-depth information on playing overtones, check out *Top Tones for the Saxophone*, a wonderful book by Sigurd M. Rascher.

B.

C.

D.

E.

F.

G.

H.

I.

CHAPTER 16
TRANSPOSITION

"Why am I in a different key from the rest of the band?" This is a common question from anyone who has just bought a saxophone, taught themselves a little bit, and then decided to play with some other musicians. It can be a big shock to discover that the keyboard player, the guitar player, and the bass player are all playing in the key of C, so when you join in with your alto or tenor sax, you get dirty looks because you are in a completely different key.

Saxophones are transposing instruments. That's why the alto and baritone are in the key of E♭ and the soprano and tenor are in the key of B♭. These designations tell you what note a specific sax has to play to match the concert pitch – to line up with the instruments that are non-transposing, such as the piano, bass, and guitar mentioned above. For example, if the piano plays a C, the alto/bari have to play A and soprano/tenor have to play a D.

To be more specific, the alto has to play down a minor 3rd plus an octave (or up a major 6th) to match concert pitch, baritone up a major 6th plus and octave (major 13th), tenor up a major 2nd plus an octave (major 9th), and soprano up a major 2nd.

Transposing music on the spot takes practice. Like anything, the more practice you do, the easier and faster it becomes. Try this:

1. First, determine what key the C part is in, then do the proper "key" transposition to figure out the new key. In the first example below, the concert key is F major; transpose the B♭ part up a major 2nd and the E♭ part down a minor 3rd.

2. For B♭, practice reading the C part up a whole step, remembering what key you're in. Later, when you are more comfortable with the notes and transpositions, the tenor part can play up an octave (most of the time just adding the octave key).

3. Alto and baritone, practice reading down a minor 3rd, remembering what key you're in. Then when you're more comfortable with the right notes, practice adding the octave key, which will be the correctly transposed notes.

When practicing these basic transpositions, cover up the B♭ and E♭ parts to quiz yourself, then check to see if you're correct. Practice piano accompaniments parts to greatly improve your transposition reading.

ACKNOWLEDGMENTS

I would like to offer special thanks to the following people: Jeff Schroedl, Hal Leonard Corporation; all the great teachers I've had: Conrad Zemke, Curt Hanrahan, Jim Riggs, John Webb, Rob Rose, David Lewis, Steve Jones, Steve Wiest, Jeff Clayton, Dan Higgins; my parents; my wife April; my wonderful children, Nathan and Ava.

ABOUT THE AUTHOR

Eric J. Morones hails from Racine, WI. He attended the University of Wisconsin-Whitewater, where he received a degree in communications, with a minor in music. He later did graduate work in jazz studies at the University of North Texas. Now living in Los Angeles, Eric has played, toured, and/or recorded with Kelly Clarkson, the Brian Setzer Orchestra, Big Bad Voodoo Daddy, Bobby Caldwell, Steve Tyrell, Maureen McGovern, Jack Sheldon, Bill Holman, Will Kennedy, and Chad Wackerman. His sax playing is featured on the *Big Fish Audio Sample DVD Suite Grooves 1 and 2*. He has performed at the Montreux and North Sea Jazz Festivals, as well as on *The Tonight Show with Jay Leno, Dancing with the Stars, Late Night with Conan O'Brien, The Today Show, Live with Regis and Kelly,* and *Woodstock '99*.

A busy author, Eric has written the books *101 Saxophone Tips, Paul Desmond Saxophone Signature Licks, 25 Great Saxophone Solos,* and *25 Great Trumpet Solos* (Hal Leonard Corporation). He wrote a bi-monthly column for the *Saxophone Journal* called "From the Front Lines," and produced two Masterclass CDs for the magazine: *How to Play Pop, R&B and Smooth Jazz* and *How to Play the Blues*. Eric's first solo jazz CD, *About Time!*, is available on Arabesque Records.

ericmorones.com

HAL•LEONARD SAXOPHONE PLAY-ALONG®

The Saxophone Play-Along™ Series will help you play your favorite songs quickly and easily. Just follow the music, listen to the CD to hear how the saxophone should sound, and then play along using the separate backing tracks. Each song is printed twice in the book: once for alto and once for tenor saxes. The melody and lyrics are also included in the book in case you want to sing, or to simply help you follow along. The audio CD is playable on any CD player but it can also be used in your computer to adjust the recording to any tempo without changing pitch!

1. ROCK 'N' ROLL

Bony Moronie (Larry Williams) • Charlie Brown (The Coasters) • Hand Clappin' (Red Prysock) • Honky Tonk (Parts 1 & 2) (Bill Doggett) • I'm Walkin' (Fats Domino) • Lucille (You Won't Do Your Daddy's Will) (Little Richard) • See You Later, Alligator (Bill Haley) • Shake, Rattle and Roll (Bill Haley).

00113137 Book/CD Pack...$16.99

2. R&B

Cleo's Mood (Junior Walker & the All-Stars) • I Got a Woman (Ray Charles) • Pick up the Pieces (Average White Band) • Respect (Aretha Franklin) • Shot Gun (Junior Walker & the All-Stars) • Soul Finger (The Bar-Kays) • Soul Serenade (King Curtis) • Unchain My Heart (Ray Charles).

00113177 Book/CD Pack...$16.99

3. CLASSIC ROCK

Baker Street (Gerry Rafferty) • Deacon Blues (Steely Dan) • The Heart of Rock and Roll (Huey Lewis & the News) • Jazzman (Carole King) • Smooth Operator (Sade) • Turn the Page (Bob Seger) • Who Can It Be Now? (Men at Work) • Young Americans (David Bowie).

00113429 Book/CD Pack...$16.99

4. SAX CLASSICS

Boulevard of Broken Dreams (Sam Butera) • Harlem Nocturne (Sam "The Man" Taylor) • Night Train (Jimmy Forrest) • Peter Gunn (Henry Mancini) • The Pink Panther (Henry Mancini) • St. Thomas (Sonny Rollins) • Tequila (The Champs) • Yakety Sax (Boots Randolph).

00114393 Book/CD Pack...$16.99

HAL•LEONARD® CORPORATION

7777 W. BLUEMOUND RD. P.O. BOX 13819 MILWAUKEE, WI 53213

Visit Hal Leonard online at **www.halleonard.com**